B.N. Lawson

XXII:

Metamorphoses

North Carolina

JOSIE'S GUILD, L.L.C.

Copyright © 2024 by B.N. Lawson
www.bnlawson.com

Cover Art © [Jasper & Fern](#), 2024
Photography © [Rebecca Emilson](#), 2023
Hairstyling by Whitney Sapp at [Dye Pretty](#), 2024
Editing by Erin Hodge at [They're, Their, There Editing](#)

All rights reserved. This book or any portion thereof
may not be reproduced or used in any manner whatsoever
without the express written permission of the publisher
except for the use of brief quotations in a book review.
The Publisher is not responsible for websites
(or their content) that are not owned by the Publisher.

Library of Congress Control Number: 2024902005

Printed in the United States of America
First Edition, 2024
ISBNs 9798989934133 (hardcover)
9798989934171 (paperback)

Josie's Guild, L.L.C.
200 Dick St. Ste D #105
Fayetteville, NC 28301-5720
[www.josiesguild.com](#)

To my health care team,
thanks for your compassion and persistence.

To Authorites,
thanks for listening.

To the Catholic Church,
thanks for making room for me.

To my Chosen Family,
you are my world even when I'm lost in mine.
I love you.

To my Littles,
you are my ever-burning passion.
I love you.

To my Love,
my Exodus, my Moon, the Glorious Star
illuminating my nights; I love you.

~

Voy con Dios, Papá.
I miss you.

PREFACE

XXII: Metamorphoses contains seven Books with seventy-three poems, inspired by Greek mythology. The first five Books are: Depression, Denial, Anger, Bargaining, and Acceptance. The last two Books are: Hope and Triumph. Each book contains elements of psychological and spiritual metamorphosis -- to my detriment and benefit. While I didn't set out to create a Hero's Journey, I did -- a Psychological Hero's Journey. Each book stands independently and flows with the next one. There is a glossary in the back with vocabulary and all the Greek Mythology references. If you would like to read *XXII:* with music, I have created a Spotify Playlist.

This epic is a victorious soliloquy for that twenty-two year old part of me that got to write the ending of the play in which she was reluctantly cast. She fought bravely in an extremely dangerous situation. I am immensely proud of her — proud of me. Reacquainted in 2022 with incredible pain, she is me and I am her. XXII: offers an explanation on how I related to an unspeakable grief caused by a crucifiable "faith". ***Across the pages, there will be themes of violence, sexual assault, violations, and severe mental health struggles. Tread carefully through the pages, caring for your own heart and mind.*** You may feel the mayhem and madness, but I promise the darkness only paints deep shadows behind the most beautiful, glorious Eden. My greatest hope is that the Reader can embark on their own personal epic, finding solace, resolution, and healing from misery (missourie in my world). Transform the treachery with me and tell yourself how wonderful and lovely you are — shadows, pain, and all.

JANE DOE *by* B.N. LAWSON

These trembling hands are not the first to jostle
away unholy grabs from praying hands;
you crossed the lines Christ drew in coastal
sands before the crowd gathering their stones.
You blamed me for it all.

Possessed with fierce rapacity, you blurred
the lines—ransacking my temple, breaking doors,
all the drawers and boards of floor; finding stores
of compunctious grief to circumfuse your sins,
leaving my honor tousled.

Your honor intact—down to my knees, I fall;
my shame on full display in boxes of glass:
sore hips, bruised thighs, crying "God's good will."
I'll confess it all in tattered clothes,
offering up these last lines—

drawn cross my hurting hands worn from survival,
splayed out as infinitesimal steep ravines,
where creeks of tears flow cross a fleshly live
terrain; washing away all of his sins,
slipping past stained fingers—

tips thudding glass and hoping to be seen,
but all that anyone sees are just frail shadows
in this vast opaque sea of Jane Does beneath
ceilings tall we sought to shatter, but we're
silenced by their secrets.

Banging fiercely, this glass box must fall.
Ravines of lines crossed within all our fists
that you cannot control—cause after all,
when we break this glass, we'll create windows
with bright and glorious panes—

casting light on our faces as you fall
from grace, knowing Jesus Christ drew lines
where we now stand—answering the call
to proclaim truth to a crowd dropping stones:
that all of us were raped.

Published by The Society of Classical Poets, March 2024

BOOK I
DEPRESSION
I - XII

*XIII | Abandoned | Garden o' Carolina | Don't Thank Me. |
Set the Stage | Raven | Liar | Maimed Muliebrity |
Valley o' Missourie | Laborers | I'm in Deep. | Dogs of War*

BOOK II
BARGAINING
XIII - XXIII

*On My Own | Rumplestiltskin | Silver | Carried Away |
The Death of Faith | Ashes to Ashes | Je T'aime | The Fae's Thimble
| Railtrack | Andromeda | Laurel*

BOOK III
ANGER
XXIV - XXXVII

*Icarus | Canaan | Meteor Shower | Starship | Throne |
Meadow of Mayhem | Honey Badger | Bemoaned | Martyr |
Forsaken | Damned | Iota | Chione's Demise | AP --*

BOOK IV
DENIAL
XXXVIII - XLVII

*Bear My Burdens | Haunted | Somniphobia | No. | Leviathan |
Serpents | Blood in the Water | In Theory... | The Box |
My Obsidian Night*

BOOK V
ACCEPTANCE
XLVIII - LVII

*Lucifer, Lucifer! | Waxing Crescent | Hold'n You All Close. |
The Dead Don't Speak | Apollyon Falls | False Arcadia | Tartarus |
Washed Ashore | The Black Cat | Time.*

BOOK VI
TRIUMPH
LVIII - LXVI

*Dawn of the Devil | Mephistopheles | Careful, Now... |
It's All a Game (to you) | The End is Neigh | Sojourners | :XXII |
Grave Robber | The Fire*

BOOK VII
HOPE
LXVII - LXXIII

*Alchemy | Holy Grail | Mise-en-scéne |
Bouquet from the Forest Floor | The Final Banquet |
Charybdis / Scylla | Chosen*

ENCORE
cxxi - cxxviii

Selah | Dear, Reader. | Glossary

"Holy places are dark places. It is life and strength,
not knowledge and words, that we get in them. Holy wisdom
is not clear and thin like water, but thick
and dark like blood."

- C.S. Lewis, *Till We Have Faces*

BOOK I

XIII

Cradle laid bare before a Mother unknown,
borne to her in sorrow, two decades past.
All I've done is run, tripping over loathsome
roots, a morass against aching ankles.

The breeze in the trees unfurling
the branches as sails set to Pacific winds;
I fall beneath men's secrets that flutter
to the forest floor like Autumn leaves.
I'd hoped to fall beneath it all, buried
to death, a wisp of a life never lived,
only wasted. Parched, maimed, and
starved, I could no longer rise and run.

It was then a sunrise broke the night;
hues of Aubergine and Orange blanket
my bed of machiavellian mendacities.
A magnificent mirth warms my face.
This Truth is inalienable, undeniable!
This Sun rose over a fertile forest
floor after decades of death
and I rose like English Ivy.

Stumbling out of the forest
onto Holy cobblestone, I fell
in humble, grieved submission.
Oh, blessed El Camino, I'll walk now.
That nickname I carried since my youth
suited me well. I was a Bucket brimming
with murky water that was dumped
out, washed clean, and made anew
in the early morning hours.

Murky water trickled over
pebbles and stones beneath
The Virgin and Job's Coffin;

shining bright, in Heavenly
Waters I'm now perfected with.

Look, I'm within my Mother's sight!
I'm borne again into Christ's arms;
Warm and Loving, Joy bloomed
and I discovered where Home was.
The desire to love others consumed
until someone said I can't.

Tripped right from the cobblestone
into a net woven of prevarications,
cast by false fishers of women.
What was meant to be a swathing
network of safety was actually
for prey, entangling me in depravity.

What was washed anew became
soiled and dented as it was thrown
from hand to hand in haste.
My purpose was indiscernible,
unknown to eyes most unholy.

The Cobblestone laid bare,
they took this Bucket and beat me
into a footrest for the devil in the name
of a Holy Sovereign who would
never cease His pursuit,
crying out for me by a
name only He knew.

ABANDONED

Gushing wounds,
mud beneath my nails,
sorrows saturate my wails.
False Fishers cast me into
a grave dug just for me
with a blank tombstone.

Do you see me?
Can you hear me?

Anyone?

Delirious with desperation,
what was a wolf I welcomed
as a savior. Soft paws, clean fur,
pristine teeth that nipped me where it hurt,
dragged me from the sacred safety only a grave
could offer, into the night with creatures vile;
gashed wide open before the Devil's
Dawn where I was left to die before
a crowd that couldn't see the wolves.

I tried my damndest.
Promised to be Esther,
but I was Gomer, deservingly.
I hid my pain and that was wrong.
Thus, I proved myself a manipulative,
lying whore instead of a queen,
earning my new name:

Jezebel.

GARDEN O' CAROLINA

Lo, a gathering of sad cheer
in Garden o' Carolina, an Eden
of sorts swooning with amor.
Alas, all this love is bidding me
adieu to a valley far off.

Please, don't send me away.

The candle worn down, barely a flicker;
the bird's gusts blew it out in the night,
thrown across the expanse, out of sight
away from my first home and family.

Please, don't send me away.

I was English Ivy deeply Rooted,
growing amongst the most serene,
sweet aromas, singing glorious praise —
ever-reaching for the Son who never scorched.
From fertile ground, I was yanked and
cast away beneath unbearable heat.

What woulda been living
was now dying.
What shoulda bloomed
all fell away as I flew.
What coulda been beautiful was
flung west to pander a bawd.

English Ivy withered, taken
over by ivy poison, infecting
everything she touched.

Please, take me back.

DON'T THANK ME.

Delicate demur mattered not.
Broad hand caressed my hip.
Just past the small of my back
in that cramped, small space.

You whispered frightening nothings
to my ear as if it's yours to taint.
Adulterine hegemony.
I never wanted this!

Vermillion shame swept across my face
as a dusting of bloodstained snow.
Hunted as prey, you knew I had to stay,
Giving Thanks to you and your wife.
I'm frigidly affright, she's three steps away.
Felt you step back, crawled inside myself.
Make no eye contact and vow to never
partake in Thanksgiving again.

Friendsgiving be damned, I'll miss
that candle-lit wood floor back home.
Cheeks pricked by ice on my lone walk.
You take what you want and
leave nothing left.

Demur be damned as I was
that dark night of diablerie
just beyond the kitchen.

SET THE STAGE

I paid his price and I set flight,
straight to a hanging rock.
Stood upon the ledge bereft
amongst a Northern Flock.
My loved ones held my wrist,
but I still had to watch my back.

That Devil's Dawn was a spotlight;
she made me play the liar.
The Devil counted clocks 'til midnight;
He made me play the lover.
The Devil's mistress wrote the script;
She made me play enchanter.

Desperately alone on stage,
I wanted to burn the page,
but, I must say all is well
because if I dared to tell…

Your doubt would build my casket
because you all were all I had
and all I had would burn up fast.
I am the catch, 22; bemoan my fate;
trapped between the desperate maws
of your Scylla and his Charybdis,
I tried so hard. Yea, I broke both legs;
I played the roles of survival,
in his bed, immured by the Bible.

RAVEN

Caged bird, I was a raven,
dead in trespasses not my own.
Flew back to you with secrets
that unraveled beneath the wine glass
I perched atop, diving in too often.
But I spoke a foreign language
I learned in my cage,
Never able to say *more*.

I owed him for this blessed trip,
indebted to the one who ensnares me.
Never would I find solace in
a tipped glass, their arms,
nor yours even *more* so.

In my stupor, I told you of
that diabolical night in a way
only a raven could: with strategy
and caution, planning for a future
where I'd *never* be able to see
more than where I'd flown.

In the chill beneath the stars,
a rock, my perch for a moment's time.
Startled by familiarity, I swooped down
to sands that stopped me mid-flight.
Never had I seen that look as
I cried out my call of defeat.
More lies as I buried my truth.
Many things should've been said,
But all I could say was:

Never do that again.

Nevermore get close to pain
I'm unable to comprehend.

Nevermore frighten me
as my master did every day.
Nevermore tempt me to
provoke he who could pillage
this city and burn up my home.

I'll never know what would've been
had I been braver and stronger.
For now, I'll knock upon their door,
an ever-present threat forevermore.

LIAR

So, let us begin the game of this sovran,
wherein my soul becomes fractured.
All I wanted was to make it all fine
as the door shutting echoed in my mind.

Shadows enmeshed up on a ledge;
takin' up space; he crossed the line,
my sanity now waning in the wind,
I'm teetering over this edge.

The commandments carved upon the rock
crumble beneath my feet as I slip away
into the heart of Tartarus where it's dark.
They clipped my wings; I lost my way.
His warmth burns up my soul and psyche.
The winds of her wrath freeze my body.

You're a cold and stoic necromancer
divining knowledge never due to you.
Suffocate the air with enthralling,
seductive charm and douse me blue.
Darken my neurons with illusions
of grandeur that idolize you.
Take the breath from my lungs
and my soul from my bones.
Watch me crumble 'neath the lies,
believing it's oxygen — *let me breathe!*

A snake's tongue is sooner honest.
Apate must inspire these devious
musings in your itching ears,
but it is desperation desecrating me.
Here's my broken, bleeding heart.
I am yours — I am his — I am god's,
but never mine — agh, *please let me be!*

Professing unholy pomp pleasantries,
you prophesy my life to me.
Driving talons where it hurts,
I'm dragged to mystical mayhem,
a cacophony of clamoring chaos.

Wo, I need silence, let me think.

Chronos winked, now, I must confess,
this truth lacerates me, invokes your wrath,
screeching wraith, you'd take it all.
Achilles' heel was in my knees;
here, before you, I will confess
the gravest untruth of all…

I am   a liar.

MAIMED MULIEBRITY

Dear devil, I'll be your advocate.
Pulchritudinous prime of my life —
an irresistible treasure, she said as much.
I was a redemptive queen,
perfect maiden for a king of pagans.
Whispered nothings and secrets,
Wo, did Aphrodite bestow a crown,
unbeknownst to me, of scarlet red?
Nay, no one is to blame but me, *right?*

My daddy taught me well what a father's love is.
Here you are, heart of one, I offer myself up for
but a glance of grace — mere scraps of
love at your feet, as the dog.

Forbidden linens were all too tantalizing,
feeding unquenchable longings of grandeur.
Was it that or was it the lone heart I adorned?
Tsk. Tsk. Should've heeded your words: tame
my tongue, lose my soul, tchotchkes don't talk back.

You and the Sovereign put me here betwixt
these hands, so you say, I ought to raise mine with thanks.
Oh, please, forgive this soul, fuchsia frustrated your fantasies,
longing to be plucked. Never a flower, shoulda known better.

How'd I look through those binoculars that morning?
My hips a river through snow dusted mountain peaks;
I'm a goddess dusted white, twisting your name up in
the snow. My damsel desires must've burned you up.

I'm a consuming fire — irresistible delectable,
destructive force to your good, revered name.
Forget my lifelong dance, needed your dance instead.
My daydream come true to be conquered by you.
In it all, I was your fall, down into

Hade's humble abode.

Oy vey.

Man just cannot help himself
when graced with such beauty.
Even though I cut away all my glory,
wailed in agony, pushed you away.
Never mind my muddied eyes staring
back at yours with desperate pleas.
Ignore the cessation of jubilation
in my favorite time of year.
Forced thanks giving, then I'll
prop my doors and say I'm sorry,
it was all my fault for failing
to defend you from me. *Ack!*
Just bury me in the meadow.
Better had I been unborn
than to be a beauty grown,
maître d' dressed up
in you, pining
for besmirched
sweet nothings,

and this special

treatment

as your

whore....

VALLEY O' MISSOURIE

Laid beneath Reseda, brushed it with
tips so tired, nature's dander peeling,
scattering 'cross my body yellow flecks.
Like canaries falling, counted by the Holy.
Is He collecting this pain — these tears
— beneath this blistering sun?

Heaven, help me, save me now,
bury me among the mignonette,
my body be marred no more.
Sweet wafts of relief, I do beg and
clamor with haste to my Mother
unknown, hear these petitions:
to you I wished to soar
beyond this Valley o' Missourie
where groans hide illicity,
grins conceal depravity
enduring labor unseen.

Oh, please, Lord, I beseech thee,
bestow mercy unto me.
Let las gallinas crow and
horses whinny my gospel.
I am but an ass, but these
creatures loved 'round just
might provoke humility.

Nay, snakes bear the bullet,
raise a cleaver to my chickens,
and suffocate mice in bleach
with our grief shaken hands.

Can I be sure I don't face
the butcher or a bullet?

LABORERS

Making mountains out of moments
that never mattered to anyone but us,
ricocheted remorse reverberated my
blistered cheekbone beneath your hand.
Chills of ecstasy trickled through vertebrae
constringed by the weight of my shame.

This excruciation was rapturous from
your fields of laboring votaries,
awaiting a Holy Rapture beneath Blood
Moons with clenched and clamoring fists.
Dulcet grins orchestrating an apocalypse,
escort hands where they oughtn't have been
over a body, clearly, no longer my own.

I'M IN DEEP.

He ruled with Python's charm;
I gave him my clothes.
She spoke the Siren's hymn;
I gave her my thoughts.

The shores of my mind transform
and I find myself stepping through
tinkling glass like a waterfall;
it shimmers light that sings.

Grandiosity and curiosity eclipse
my good and right sense.
I ceased considerations of my
impending consequence.

Deep breath, take it all in;
inhale the aromatic escape
awaiting me so we can begin
the feast — your main course.

This acacia adorned banquet
hosts strangers and serpents
here to become my family.
They hide their intent behind
clouds yanked from the sky,
set out as fresh linens to dine.
Dinner is served by lumières:
the potter's finest lamb and
potatoes of our calloused hands.
The air around me swims with
sounds of the harp and lyre.

Dive deep into my mind,
I'm a beauty amongst beasts.
Cover me in black and muddy
sackcloth. Then, cast me to the

creek of lost souls, I am one with them.
My body writhes in ecstatic laughter.
Tears of pain flow over gasps for air.
Feet pinned down by the imps,
an angel like an angler fish,
bright as Lucifer when he fell,
enamors me and I sink.

Woe, no. My soul is the feast.

What was riveting rived my soul with
sharp cuts and perplexing confessions.
I'm covered in shame; drowned in confusion.
The belly of the angler is no place to be;
the pain won't stop; it won't spit me out.

The hymns harm me; the venom stings.
Angels on High, defend me, please!

DOGS OF WAR

A knock upon the metal gate,
the ting creates an echo of plaints.
The sound clenches my chest —
I'm barely breathing from the pain
of working for your worthless gain.
Woe, lament my conundrum!
Cerberus and its dogs snarl and howl,
ever keeping me in subdued control.
To bend to your will, I must break
myself by way of Word-fare
proclaimed a fair and worthy war
conquering saint-less selves:

Carve out those intuitions;
trust the lying dogs.
*Provide for them, or be
damned at the denial of your faith.*

Tears of iron weigh heavy on sullen cheeks,
bruising them with grief never allowed —
*Without a grumble for a mere crumble
of falsely promised grace, I do all things.*

Don't buckle — Cerberus is on the hunt.
Force my calloused hands to work and
Never rebuke an older man, He is your father.

One can make a horse believe it's a bee,
so long as its trained well enough.
Such is the truth for my own soul,
making myself believe I deserve this.
Icy fractals fill my lungs as I inhale
to cease the crying, hold the horses.
Alas, I'll find comfort in the other beasts
of this field — beautiful, majestic, Happy.

Swept up in chestnut are your passions
in the cold of dawn as you hoist hay.
I abhor the grin detailing unholy lusts.
I'm inflamed with fury and fright —
these libidinous observations
of my maidenhood bring
about the ass in me.
I bite back —

— and you devour.
Swept up in rage are your passions,
setting fire to my portrait as I stand here
and burn but refuse to fall into your lap
a violent, silent victory.

In the tapestry of my life,
Sovereignty must be weaving deep
shadows beneath curtains scooping
up all my pain into these odious hands
to drop it behind me so I bow
in a finale you orchestrate.

What she said was a movie theater
is a play and I am your puppet.
Stringing the lines I must cross down
my chest with a piercing threat:

I'd hate for them to find out.
Best you keep it quiet.

Oy vey, **fuck you.**
Shakespeare is weeping,
strings snap as I won't bend,
the curtain is aflame as it drops.
What a loathsome end of me!
Not a tragedy nor a comedy,
just a woeful injustice.
I'll hold my head high,

bravely before Lucifer's gaze
in a territorial stalemate,
I won't show you I'm petrified.
No, I'm fortified by
a silent soliloquy of sorts:

"My resolve is fierce —
Lo, a box I tuck this moment.
He has made me an Impious Pandora,
all our secrets wrapped up maroon
will spill out through time,
across this Holy tapestry wherein
The Creator creates beauty
of his ill-fated depravity."

BOOK II

ON MY OWN

I became Pandemonium;
clouds gathered in my head,
and like a besieging wind,
my words threatened his throne.
The hands of my god gripped
my arm and all my uproar
shuddered before his face.
Sorrow soaked the clouds
as he warned me well that
he alone authored two tales.

Truth is held by those with power:
I am the Harlot, I am the Betrayer.
It was I who was the temptation;
this life, this loss was all my fault.
I may very well bear his fruit, but
it was I who stole his secrets.

This storm turned silver,
with no lining to be found
as my price to pay increased.
So, I built a boat with all new
machiavellian mendacities.
Setting sail and taking flight
I took matters into my own,
lonely and desperate hands.

RUMPLESTILTSKIN

Perched atop the pigs, I stared at you and you at me.
Prey against her predator, a dove fluttered by with palm.
Oh, hold the hope, is this raven doomed to fall?
Wanted to pluck the envelope from your hands and
read what you could hold me hostage with.
Alas, like freedom, this too was a forbidden
treat, tucked away in a pocket blue and worn.

What coulda been blackmail was
a tether 'gainst my hidden will.
Gave up my trinkets and futures
as he baulked while I flew East
for Spring, carrying with me
straw promised to turn gold to
build a nest and make a
treasure kept.

Gingerly, tenderly, I laid them
out piece by piece, planning and
shifting to accommodate my needs.
Gold promised never showed and
in the desperation, I tried to swim,
but as I dove, that tether yanked
me from the sky back west
through prismatic falls
to a potter's field
with baroque walls
and silver debts.

SILVER

The cost of betrayal fell
with me to the floor.

Alone I wondered my chances.
Flip that silver, spin it well.
He said, two sides to every tale.
Heads, it's yes — perhaps I'll live.
Tails, it's no — perhaps I'll die.

New life, give life —
this one's gonna take mine.
I cannot bear a beauty
just to burn it up.
I'd hoist it in the air,
a casualty of the war
that laid me bare.
Hands so holy stained
unholy all to sacrifice
this life just to ruin his.

Make a vow, keep his secret.
Juno can hold her wrath.
Spin that silver, let it fall.
Merciful mayhem, your
musing's as good as mine.

CARRIED AWAY

Perhaps it was a love I kept myself from?
— perhaps it never was and 'twas freedom's grasp?
Hands hold this body in a scene most lonesome;
silenced in agony, I can only weep.

Don't tell me it's off in Christ's arms asleep —
Just bury me out back; the slope to Hell's steep.
All because of man and his transgressions unwelcome —
— perhaps it never was and 'twas freedom's grasp?

I would've stayed there, unable to escape
this place, forgoing comfort in Christ's arm.
I'd like to think it was just mayhem,
caused by man, who demands I restrain my tongue.
Perhaps it was a love I kept myself from?

Perhaps it was a love I kept myself from?
My tongue restrains his secrets most loathsome.
I'd like to think it was just mayhem,
never a soul upheld by Christ's arm.
I would've stayed there, unable to escape.

— perhaps it never was and 'twas freedom's grasp?
Borne of some man and his transgressions unwelcome —
I'll bury it out back in my mind; the hill's steep.
Don't you tell me it's off in Christ's arms asleep!

Silenced in agony, I can only weep.
Hands hold this body in a scene most lonesome;
— perhaps it never was and 'twas freedom's grasp.
Perhaps it was a love I kept myself from.

THE DEATH OF FAITH

Laying hollow on the floor,
all I craved was the aubergine
Love that Graced me orange
that mirthful Autumn morn.
When time reset, once again borne.
I reached for every good thing above
instead of longing for my grave.

And when the Devil's Dawn swept
in, there was a collision of careful
colors across my skies as You fought
away all her lies and her false light.
Through it all, I felt known and kept.

Each color was carefully painted
over me as if I was Your new canvas.
All that gray was blanched floral white
The white spaces filled up with amaranth.
You set a table draped in pickle and purple.
Ebony faded behind the brightest cobalt.
Your Aubergine and Orange held them all
and by your Hands, something New appeared.

But, my canvas needed layer upon
layer to cover darkened places.
No matter how New I thought I was,
the old shadowed the bright colors
spread over my broken frame.

Yea, I broke both legs
and wore a shattered heart.
It was truly just too much.

Cruel as Kindness shipped me West —
he took a razor to Your canvas;
cut me out of frame and hung me

'bove his bed like a taxidermy token.
I became the talking point 'round
their fields of moving targets.
He flicked his wrist; a furious red.
I bore the fruit of his lascivious labor.
You showed up to create life, but
never once showed up to save mine.
They fired holes through me,
spraying Your canvas with shades
of maroon, tinted black and blue.
— and Love and Grace finally left.

Why paint me aubergine when
You knew he would stain it blue?
Why shade me orange when
You knew he would tint it black?
Why did You paint me anew when
You knew he would bear his mark?

Tally the clocks and set the dogs;
I was up for auction and I paid
the price that forlorn midnight;
the buyer burned Your canvas
and You'll never find the ashes.

ASHES TO ASHES

I'm haunted by my own shadow.
She holds his secrets and taunts me.
Let's play God and hoist Death's Scythe.
I'll gladly take my worthless life;

All these false promises
covered me with a door of teak
and his love nailed it shut.
She was me and I was her.
I forsake the part of me that
was strong and brave.

Shut the lid on this season;
slam it tight upon my soul!
This pain has left me undone.
All I can do is weep and wail.
Reaching in, deep within,
I rip my shadow and I fall
away down by the creek
as my darkness stood close.

I awakened in the night
where I and all was lost.
Avoiding him created a void.
Within seconds, a black hole emerged.
Failure flung me here, but it was
I who failed to fight my way back.
With everything and everyone to lose;
I arise a ghost of myself, dressed black.
Half a soul; I would never be free.
I took flight with corpse white
knuckles suffocating truth,
clenching onto all the lines
that strung his secrets into

little white lies.

JE T'AIME

Marionette beneath gentle hands.
Watch me work and twist myself —
toss a penny, a gratuity to repair the cracks
and broken strings after his gentle hands
needed more than I could offer.

Terrifying sonatas were his whispers
wafting minty notes of instruction to
bend me to his wicked will with a smile
and a show for the world.

With every turn, my arms raise out
as a graceful, blushing beauty beloved.
Entertaining him well, I'd hear the
kindest laugh in the chill, warming
these brittle, breaking limbs.

Draws near, caressing joints tender,
cheeks inflamed, soft with sorrow soaked
up by empty promises and frightening
secrets to keep me bound to a Christian crossbar.

Could hardly stand the intensity of his
gaze — a gravitational pull into him
as I hung above the stage, begging for a
morsel of his mercy and grace.

Broad and strong, he finesses my
broken strings, tugging on unhealed crevices
'cross a wooden face rotting from the tears
above the smile she made me show.

After all, love without strings is dead. *Right?*

THE FAE'S THIMBLE

I was flung west as English Ivy,
but the poison took over and
something new fell abloom,
by that muddy creek, baby.

I'm Foxglove grown in muddy waters.
Beauty adorns my embittered spite.
My fingers are all stained fuchsia.
If you look inside, you'll see some white
speckled with dark spots of remorse
that look better in the Light.

Only blooms in the sun with a love
so potent that it's got the power
to heal and kill the unlucky beholder.
They say I'm the witches' glove,
the foxes' footings, the fae's thimble;
protection for the wily and wise.

Inhale the aroma and pull me close,
but never too close! — pure digitalis
runs through each and every vein.
I'll break your heart with a high dose,
but just enough will restart your heart.

It hangs around you in the air so thick
you can't see what comes next.
Hold me tight, *but not too tight!*
I'll slip through your grasp just
to toss my whims into the windbreak
and flutter back to my old gallant.

Flowers bloom where they're planted
and I came back to you in a mason jar.
Beau, be the garden I can't seem to find.
Tolerate the digitalis and test the water;

there's bound to be a cure we can find.
Entangle our Roots; I'll reach down further
and break through the glass just to be held.

We can sway in the moonlight all summer;
stay with me a while, *but not too long!*
The bane of my presence is that I hurt and I heal.
Digitalis is my known reality, but I've yet
gazed into clean water to understand *why*.

RAILTRACK

Love is fair and love is fine,
but mine construed blurred lines.
The only candle I held was the one
to your chest, burning up reason.
Nay, we neglect what I said,

I'm going back with or without you.

Metal wheels against those tracks;
so too, were my words as they hovered
above the candlelight, lingering too long,
railing against every good thing in you.

Conjuring imaginations of a vain flavor
to justify what was to come,
we set our sights on moons afar
and firmament forbidden.

I loved you a little, just not enough
to extinguish this false flame.
It woulda been doused away
by bitter rains you'd not forgotten
had you dared me to stay.

ANDROMEDA

Beneath the trees, I set my gaze above.
The Moon's wink was tinged pink.
The lull of crickets soothed my soul,
but the hauntings of my mind shuddered
my breathing, my chest gripped by
the ghost of me — she's calling.

Save yourself from this Valley;
Come back and burn it all.

I couldn't pause all these motions managed
by the strings 'round my heart and wrists.
My love can have the whole half of me.
Maybe we'll find the rest in the Valley.

I'm a damsel set to doom,
they sway and shift my mind.
We'll cast ourselves to the church
evangelizing places thirsty
and saving everyone else's world.
All because I needed saving from my own
filled with sorrow, fear, and mayhem.

By the time day broke, I ventured out and
dove deep into pig slope to find pearls.
My hands dripped mud across my dress.
I strung my white lies together; a string
of stained pearls draped around my neck.
My reflection horrendous; my season
with swine touched everything around.

But, not a soul seemed to notice.
Celebrate the bride! She isn't ready!

Beneath lavender stars and acacia walls,
we reached for Zion, attained it well enough.

Mountains moved in magical matrimony,
the Garden o' Carolina is aglow with zeal.

Let us never depart this place,
let's shift gears and move this clock back.
We'll pause and hover over what was
victorious, catching the sparks in our
skies colliding. You and I can
caress the firmament in our palms,
thrown from the expanse
just for the sake of our glance.
But, the Ghost of me whispered,

The strings must be cut.

Hold the way as Perseus.
I shine as Andromeda.
All this love was brighter
than my deepest dark.

But, darling, I made enemies and
they stood amongst us all.
Deep in the bones you behold,
I'm quietly dying while my
enemies cackle and cry out.

Darling, fight for me,
we'll carve our trail back North.
Cleave to me and never let go,
even when the monstrosity
emerges from Poseidon's wrath
and bears down on you through
hands meant to hold.

LAUREL

What I thought was an Oak was a
Laurel; indeed, and I didn't want to escape.
To bear the pain of a lone tree or embrace
these roots and draw closer to a suffering
alternative metamorphosis?

My anger inflamed me as I fell out
of control, lost, and into grave danger.
What have I done to rip us away
from home through ways of Dolos?

Tricked me into seeing Eden
when it was Pandemonium all along.
At the cross, atop that miserable
hill, I loathed myself, making
vows I ought never keep.

A Laurel I'll be, by a cross
at the creek, alone I will bear this
'cause on my own I brought
us here. With him on my mind
when I shoulda been flying
with you back home to ridges blue.

BOOK III

ICARUS

Rushing wind silenced me
as I took in my view as the Raven.
Quilted land and stunning windmills
as mere dandelions, blowing away every
hurt to the wind, as if it never was.
Energizing me to survive because
I knew it was, is, and was to come
up again when I could face it.

My dearest Icarus beneath this star,
you drew close in inharmonious matrimony.
In the sky, clear as day, I could see it as
I grabbed the wheel with shaking hands
— an end to us all in one fell swoop,
plummeting to Earth a fiery sign
of their sought after apocalypse.

Heaven help me, save us now.
Gargantuan pain, inconceivable,
has made me insane and like this plane,
my ginormous soul needs small adjustments.
Thus, I'll coast their skies, a starship waiting
to crash into them and blow it all up.

I'll make the smallest moves towards
one big moment wherein what
was, is now, and yet to come
flips this plane awry.

Fluttering secrets to the wind,
falling to Earth to taint their
land and become their undoing.
Forgive me, not for betraying
your authority, but failing
to set the plane aflame
when I could.

CANAAN

Sultry sun baked the pine.
The lilies I plucked were but stars in the sky.
Dreams of underserving grace,
hopes of freely given mercy.
I played Oizys, but now
I longed for peace.

Don't try to outrun demons.
If you do, make sure you can.
Panic makes one unpredictable.
But, so too, does Power.

Proserpina in this Canaan countryside,
Pluto, you stole my soul.
Wrenched it from my being,
cast it down to Sheol.
It was you who should've died that day.
The Good Book says as much,
but it was me that died instead.
My heart gave out, my soul gave in.
Hello, Hades, I relent.

This promised land only promised pain.
I may have reached for the flower,
but you opened the Earth.
Across the way, she didn't see my
body wrought of diabolical desire.
Anguished wails escaped to silence
'cept round the Elysian Fields
you claimed to behold.

Father of All heard my crestfallen woes
as I lay abandoned in the dirt,
my chest branded with the mark of this hell.
Seventh Circle, third wheel — *damn this 37!*
I cried out through the flames,

reach down, save this broken soul,
I'm fractured now, filleted wide open.
Your Son has been here before.
Free me from the guilt I bear:

It's all my fault — I sought the lily.
It's all my fault — I knew not to run.
It's all my fault — I returned.

Heaven help me, Holy guide.

METEOR SHOWER

Oh, my sweet relief, our Roots pulled us closer
and you lit up the sky with aura borealis.
I desired to watch your night sky evermore,
but the planets shifted, crashing into us
and we fell from grace, a meteor shower
burning up on our way down.

You no longer illuminated my sky
and I no longer burned with beauty.

This shower drenched the land
in bitter flames and all we
could do was hold weapons, welded
in self-defense, in the aftermath,
before the dust had even settled.

Blinded by it all, we could see
clearly how doomed we were.
I slipped into the Earth,
swallowed whole as I
scrambled for you, but
you never grabbed my hand.

STARSHIP

What Exodus were we celebrating
if not the impending one?
Wish upon a star, don't you dare put it
in my pocket, your dreams will only fade away.
Build a sukkah, swept with palm.
Please, don't make me go back.
This dwelling I'll enter beneath the stars,
don't you dare send me through
that door without them.
She made me go back.
Had to hold the items he
made me drop an eon ago.
Please, don't make me go back.
He stood there folding a blanket.
Please, don't make me go back.
Was this brevity an opportunity?
Did he want me again?
Please, don't make me go back.
Walked out the door,
tossed the stuff down,
slipped away the first chance I could.
Please, don't make me go back.
Manmade starship, stunning sight
beneath Centaurus. Brightest hope
amidst the Milky Way we harness.
I traced the bridge of your nose
against the dark curtain of night.
Adoration 'cross your face,
we share in this love of night.

Many o' nights have I adored
these very stars, casting my woes
to them as if the twinkles were winks
of compassion from God above.
Striking conversations with the
constellations that never talked back.

So, here and now, I start to confess,

the blankets we toss in their house
of glory ought be thrown to the fire,
ashes swept, kept and scattered…

but nay, my safe haven was always celestial,
when all along, it should've been you.
You were my exodus, the starship
bedazzling my sky, when all I could
do was rip dreams from yours.

THRONE

Thrown to the depths were
our dreams of false stars.
A foundation for their castle built
on our backs and our bones.

I toiled away over buckwheat
and beans in a dungeon beneath stone.
False king of my body, you demanded
I butcher the poultry I love most, but
the only thing I'm willing to butcher is *you*.

Adorning a scorn, I waltzed into your courtyard
like a swept breeze of locusts over the meadow,
juniper green rolling over hips you know well.
With a quivering voice before your throne,
I refuse to kiss those crooked hands,
dropping matches where I stand, but
fire didn't catch as I gazed at you.

Blatant disregard for your authority
granted me the whore's judgement,
but you left me there, instead, to pine
over my maniacal disruption,
dreading my imminent demise.

MEADOW OF MAYHEM

Ruling the lands with tusks of terror, you
threw me to the dirt for the dogs to dine.
From herds of birds to flocks of doe,
every one of us had something to take.
What was beautiful and majestic
became rabid with power as
you plowed the fields of
every good thing, naming
prices unattainable.

Across the pond, I warned you well,
the rising maniacal shrill is your song of death.
Singing the woes of all those you've crushed,
tenacity and resilience are her stripes,
beneath her claws are papers and pages,
enduring your swarms and facing centaurs,
accosting even the most monstrous beasts.
Beaded eyes stare you down as she plans
her strike with teeth that tear apart vipers,
your venom will not kill her.

Tromping through the wood and
digging up your worms, her body is
her armor and her weapon is her sage.
She knows well when it is best to scream
alone into the trees, a terror to the jackals
stalking the labors of her endless pursuit.
What you witlessly decried an opossum
was, indeed, a honey badger.

And she strikes to kill.

HONEY BADGER

Bees are abuzz over this Honey.
Curiosity captures the Badger
between you and the wall.
Threatened if I go any further,
I was determined to reveal it all.
I'll shatter this Hive, I swear.
Rage boiling in my bones as you
draw near with vengeance.
I'm your secret; nothing new.
But, now you're mine.

Bellicose passions burnished beneath
your lips — *you drive me ballistic*.
Perhaps this punishment bequeaths
me with salacious grabs at power.
I'll play your whore to burn you down.
My shame and vengeance burn me up.
— *Agh! I could kill you* —
Damnable witch left smoterlich!
Cardinals flew in from your church,
dipped in sin's tar and set afyre,
crashin' through the windows,
warnin' me of *my* devils afoot.
— *Ack! Carpe Noctum; take it all!* —
Pleasure became your tool of persuasion
all to create some kind of cruel culpability.
But, here's the thing: I can't say yes if
I can't say no — *I **had** to play cruel*.

I'll accept Pan's judgment, by your hands.
So, cast my parts across your Valley;
mutilate me with prongs and throw
me down into a bed of sweet potatoes
and starving mice, instead of yours.
Echoing your sins, I'll sink away.
Bury me, so I don't destroy him.

BEMOANED

Seething rage and toiling talons
set against the only one who could save
me from this meadow of mayhem.
What made me wail at night was
more precious to protect than
your heart that beat wide open.

Woe to me, this self-serving beast!

What wretched inclination I harbor
against the other part of me —
wantonly destroying us in self-defense.
I vowed to be held and loved, but
instead, all I've done is tear and gnash.
'Tis a lovely affair, all shades of promise,
an incredibly foolish endeavor, indeed.
Trees bear what they breed and, honey,
we bore something acrimoniously tart.

What is a man to do with a raging
woman but hide himself from her wrath?
Behold, cry a lamentation, our Roots died.
I wanted to be a beauty beloved,
but Honey, I'm a beauty bemoaned
bearing down on you with hands heavy.

MARTYR

Oh, bewail my rumination;
loathe my long-suffering.
You think I'm not exhausted?
Carry on about me as the burden;
but the only burden is *him* packing
me to the fucking brim with contraptions
he welded to dismantle Your canvas.

Don't try and Save me if you
deem my Suffering all too arduous.
Drop your glue and tape if you
can't tolerate the deplorable tears.
Don't you dare say I love you
if the hate I harbor horrifies.

Throwing punches in the sunlight,
I've cried and wailed to no avail;
they have burned hell into my heart.
This Bride made herself ready, alright,
for that pyre in missourie; *I'm woeful*.
They taught me how to hate
myself and blame it all on You
because suffering him was my fate,
my sanctimonious sanctification;
Athena welding spears straight
into her own heart; I'm losing
all the battles in a war that can't
be won, 'cept beneath his white flag.

So, my words cut like razors.
This Hope suffocates my truth.
False Love keeps his secrets.
My Faith pierces me crimson
as an unnecessary martyr.
So, I held a gun to my future
and told all of you, *"don't."*

FORSAKEN

I never said yes and he never heard no.
I was the hostage, but I became the holder.
Time created a Malevolent force damned
to destroy them both and burn their kingdom
because this Holy Sovereignty seemed blind.

One hell of a thief strung up on my Cross;
I stole the plot and set myself up as savior,
reviling Jesus for His sacrifice that was for
me — the one who will never be free.

For the sake of his sorrowful
passion, have mercy on me.

My cries were trapped in my throat;
they bled out on the floor,
walked out the door,
set flight to run,
burned up in the sun,
leapt off of cliffsides
into Hell inspired fires,
and drove away into the night.

For the sake of his sorrowful
passion, have mercy on me.

I stopped my clocks, but he counted them —
ticking time and taking chances til I gave in.
Time is just a construct for his own destruction.
Clocks were mere notions for them as a team.
He wore me out and she wore me down.
I razed eternity and burned up my home.
I shake these sands of time all alone,
but this can never be undone.

For the sake of his sorrowful
passion, have mercy on me.

'No' a thousand times wasted away
into a single, silent, vindictive *'yes.'*
Might judgement befall me without delay!
Lonesome midnight — what have I done?
Can't cry out now, so I shattered my hourglass.
No sense in keeping time or seeking a timeless
Sovereign after this betrayal of His Son.
When all was said and done, he held hot iron
to my closest companion — so, I kept quiet.
Thus, my beast branded me and cast me out.

DAMNED

He may have burned the canvas,
but she made me hold the flame.
Smothered in smoke, I sacrifice
myself on the alter of Abhor.

The hole to Hell is a vortex of rage;
I burn myself from the inside out;
and turned the gun on the one I love.
This wasn't just some unfortunate detour,
it was a diverted path to early graves.
All that Love I had burns up black;
you'll be damned to get it back.

Never knowing when to stop, I'll
finally step back now and let you breathe.
I tossed the gun and razors to the mud.
You've my word, I render myself
defenseless to you — cannot bear
to hurt us any longer; watch me burn.

IOTA

Was Holy something I merely imagined?
All the iotas of a Law I believed in —
What law are You waiting to be violated?
— I followed them with devotion —
What Holy desire must be accomplished?
— iotas as cannonballs hurled with abandon.
Was Justice something I merely conjured?

I have but one iota left.

Here's to hoping the heavy
hand of Holiness that hurt
me reaches down to help me.

CHIONE'S DEMISE

Numb and disillusioned,
I'm no longer me; I'm Chione
and my hope is in her hands.
My fingers shiver as temperatures
plummet and every single fighting chance
grows hypothermic with your ultimatum:

I'm going back with or without you.

So, I trade this woebegone land
for a bed of blue ridges.

Love was lost and our silence
screams louder than the storm.
Blinded by what you didn't know;
she set his trident to my demise
and in the rush, in that dusty room,
blood stained the snow.

I collapsed into the mud by the
tree line, as icy winds blew around
and I watched that ghost of me
blow away as my breathing ceased.

Now, my grief is white as snow,
a body bag draped across their land.
Frozen to death; I'm DOA.
Here, look upon the tag strung 'round
my heart — what does it say?

A P —

Snow that failed to cover sin
smudged the ink of her name.
'A P' — is it Apate or Apostle?
Who claims this deceased soul?

This body has been marooned
with secrets that weren't hers.
Momos, come claim your Hopeless,
soul, embittered and betrayed.

This soul bears scars and burns
from the sting of Loveless labor,
sacrificing herself on the alter
of her Nemesis all to save herself.

This woman is a forgone conclusion —
a forgotten footnote; hold that semicolon.
Keris come and claim your victory.
Faithless promises drove this one mad.
She tried to be whole because everyone
expected her to become whole.

Now, her aliases leave us in wait
before the period can be placed.
Delilah, the diabolical Betrayer.
Jezebel, the demonic Harlot.
Apate, the grand Manipulator.
She is to be pitied for her fate;
we'll call her *APOSTATE*.

BOOK IV

BEAR MY BURDENS

A knock upon the teak;
a whisper from the hill;
an echo in the moon;
My trembling hands hold
back the silent sobs.

Alone, I crumbled, fumbling,
and pawing for a family, a home,
where I'd become a stranger.
Roaring in desperation, I knew
This body wasn't safe — it
had been scared and marred.
Here and Now, I belonged to you,
but all I can think about is him.

What was blissful became
a burden, unnecessarily.
He didn't just take from me,
but everyone I touch.
I have yet to hold you in these
arms that want to save you from me.
The parts of me I needed were all
back west, stolen when I needed
them most — when you
needed them most.

My beautiful loves, you
Graciously awakened
a beast that desires change.
I must lean into my loss,
let it hurt, and find the Love
I lost and *when* I collect
the pieces of myself,

I'll give you everything
we all missed out on.

I'll fight this Hell inside
to give you Heaven.

I'll screech battle cries
'til I can love again.

Piece by piece, I will
grant you peace.

HAUNTED

Not a moon amongst the stars
in the fog, I wander graves
and wonder who they are.
Unnerving breeze against my ear
creates a cascade of creaking.
Tachycardia takes my breath.

Vacillating in the dark,
I slowly turn to see it's just an oak
outstretched, a blanket for my dead.
Peering over bark, she meets my eyes
and in a moment, we're face to face.
Affrighted by the specter, lightning strikes,
illuminating her translucent glow.
Woe, bewail her bruised vignette!

cup my ears, make the wailing cease.
she gawps and tilts her head, my mind
relives every grab that left her mark —
every cut that caressed my skin as
all the plates came crashing down.
Mother, dear, you ruined me
Over and over and now I'll
Make something of your ruins.
persevere through the alarum,
arms wide open drenched in grief,
i reach for condensation closing in.
Jostled by the worst man that ever lived.
Oppenheimer creating ticking time bombs.
Handprints pressed on my arms and thighs.
Never could I stop what made me bleed.
subdued as his miss minor against his skin
amidst the waves of my woeful grief.
i want to slip below them to fill the silence
as she dissipates, no longer trapped
down in the South.

victorious,
oh, sweet victory,
i am certainly done!
alas, nay, I forget who
established the cemetery.
Dear Father, It is you. I was just
A child; three and thirteen: your only
Daughter's love was fertile ground, ripe for
the plucking up and passing 'round. Knowing
i would give my all to be loved, slipping into oblivion,
an evil escape, keeping all these secrets safe.
an undoing of my own making, ten eons
past, I ended right where I started —
in a father's arms tender and
violent, passing from moment
to moment with graves upon graves —
but only this one is raised on high;
in a Mausoleum, I wander.

Footsteps echoing against the marble,
Tips tired trace the letters, bête noir,
and the crescent moon above it.
Dropping to the cold marble floor,
thunder roars, lulling me to sleep.

SOMNIPHOBIA

Whisked away to an underworld too
familiar, only you have done this to me.
Tossing and turning, dreaming of
river waves filling my lungs.
Between the gulps of the small waves closing
in on pockets of air, I swim upstream,
away from the Valley, but the further I get,
the current overtakes, rocks catch my boots.
I'm trapped beneath freshwater,
gasping as I sit upright, clawing
at my chest, weeping, nauseated,
with terror before a bulb that burned
out while I fought my sheets.

This is why I don't sleep.

Once the fright has settled,
anger pours as salt,
burning trails into my cheeks.
Was the trouncing of my
body insufficient for your
insatiable thirst of
unwavering imperium?
How are you not satisfied
with what you've stolen, still?
Why must you do this to me,
you iniquitous nigromaniac?!
Let my sleep alone, damn you,
and let this dead bury her dead!

Think you misunderstood
that golden rule about orphans:
Visit me *in* my affliction,
Not *become* my affliction.

Sleep was safe until you happened,
now nowhere is safe, save the grave.

Long to hold a memorial, just to
scatter your ashes instead of my own.
Maybe I'd finally sleep watching you wisp away
into the wind as my cries have all these years.
Oh, what peace that might bring.

Truthfully, I want the best for you —
be it brimstone orange or breezes green.
Whatever the case, it matters not because
all I can do then and now is sully this pillow
with my sad midnight wailings as
I drift away exhausted.

NO.

I awakened in the night
to strangers ripping away
the moon to pry apart the grave.
The clang of stone against marble
awakened a rage and Poseidon's
wrath came roaring back for revenge.
Wailing to the storm and sea,

She can never be set free!

Cold air pours from the mausoleum,
colliding with the crashing sea;
dense fogs saturate my wails.
Truth was flooding from
the graves of my heart
onto the shores of my soul.
The mists of rage and ice
distort the lightening and
in a flash, I see her silhouette.
Disoriented by the sight, I miss the
tidal wave, crashing to the shore, salt
water fills my lungs, gasping and grasping.

Drenched upon the shore,
battered by the hurricane.
I disappeared into the horizon
so long I witnessed the Earth turn.
Aurora Borealis danced above the stars.
Boötes hovered close to the sea;
I reminisced the fields I tarried.
A serpent lay before Ursa Minor;
he twinkles and roars beneath
Jupiter's sight as Hercules
closes in, reminding me
I once was a warrior —
an industrious one, but

when dawn broke through,
a cascade of dazzling hues
exposed fresh, raw wounds
from the first battle of my war
to overthrow you from my skies.

I'll keep my truth
and tell them lies.

Just.

Please

don't make
me talk.

I can't.

LEVIATHAN

                                  In the distance, a searchlight flashed.
                          You caught my gaze and from the sands,
                    I stepped out towards it; seaweed in the tide
                                snaked gently around my thighs.

                    ...you soothed the mayhem she caused

'til I was left in the dark with him…

You dropped the nets and set your boat
towards someone else's nightfall.
Leviathan sank her fangs deep into
my lone, woeful crucible.

Next time you want to rescue someone,
consider whether you can hoist the nets.

SERPENTS

Dragged around, the water surface
breaks like shat'ring glass as I gasp
for air beneath the searing pain.
This fight with myself shatters
time and all I'm left with is
the burn of betrayal.

The lot of you chose them over me.
I thought you were the heroes!
Some hold they have, since
we all know what he did.
I am a Bucket drenched black
wherein I lit your memory aflame
like you did our history.

Flashes of hungry sunlight
Break the water as the edges
of my mind slip away amidst
treacherous grins like his
hands did over my soul,
like she did my throat
when I was captive
to her sin.

All the while you
did **nothing**.

BLOOD IN THE WATER

I severed the strings
to escape this demise.
The net cinched me tight
as maroon clouded my seas.
The catch was the cause
for this death in the night.
I reach for the Light,
but, now?

I no longer care.

Light fades away, perhaps
I'll sleep now, forever
as I'm tenderly caressed
in Amphitrite's necropolis.
In the aspersing pause,
I relinquish the pearls
in peace, perhaps,
now, I can rest.

IN THEORY...

The waves are calm, my body is placid.
I can hear the vibrations in the clock hands
as they tick 'round, stringing time into a silenced
symphony. I begin to lose the passing hours
on a face frozen in waiting quintessence.

Minutes is all it took to take all my time.
Mere seconds were spent trying to discern
how to survive this slip through the waves
of parts and pieces made of his mistakes.

I'm Schrodinger's Cat lost to the sea;
can you tell me if I'm dead or I'm free?
No matter how far I cast the minutes
from my mind, there's a string between
point you and point me. It twists and it turns
me into a series of painful intermissions.

This play I've been cast in ends tragically.
Recapitulating the drama o'er all these eons,
I'll spend these last hours going back in time.
Don't you dare interfere; I'll do it myself.
After all, it's my fate I'm after.

Beginning again where I got in his car.
I'll run towards her frantically yelling stop.
Then, I'll look in her eyes and begin to declare
her fate if she decides to open that door;
only to be disrupted by an arrière-pensée;
I can't interfere and nor could they.

This freewill beget a fretful free fall into
a worthwhile redemption that is not about
me, but everyone he touched. So, I'll let her
go with only one admonition:

know with every broken bone that all this
time taken will not be wasted and I'm right
here when we're ready to pick up the pieces.

Making waves of constructive change —
I create a ripple of quarks and protons that
pull back the curtains for a plot twist finale.
I whisper a prayer, open my eyes and slip
back through the time lost beneath the sea.

THE BOX

Lo, a box with no treasure.
Nay, it holds bloodstained secrets
and prognostications of death.

*Might I offer myself the Love
I lend everyone else?*

Secrets this deep destroy the soul —
Gingerly, tenderly, I bend the binding,
open this delicate, tether bound book.
Turn the cover, the stone to my tomb.
Papers pour forth, drowning me
in hemorrhaging anamnesis,
stained pink bearing true witness
to the unspeakable… unfathomable.
Time is turning, time is moving
and these pages unravel time itself.
My Shadow escaped The Valley
through pages tucked away in a box.
Drenched maroon, I vociferate the violence
as I clamor through the dark wailing a
battle cry that echoes from the depths.
An octopus swims by beneath twinkling
Lights, awakening me as my lungs burn.
I reach for a surface unseen through
the waves, for I see now that I must
breathe because I am drowning.
I'll suffer this curse of knowing
myself, but never unto death.

Most Holy Sovereign awaited this moment
when I'd be most comforted — Holy Spirit
oxygenate me, Christ in Heaven flush
this wound, Father stitch it closed.
Holy Mother, grant me comfort,
Saints above, anesthetize me in

glimmers of Glory littering the sky.
Savior, wrest me from these waters,
grant me Peace and give me Rest.

MY OBSIDIAN NIGHT

Dear, Shadow; Dear, Shadow,
I'm drenched gray before you.
Awaken my lungs with breath anew;
enjoin my soul for our final blow.

Achilles' heel was in his hands
all along; my knees may have
buckled, but now his hold breaks.
Dear Shadow, my Obsidian Night;
shade me black, reach down
through the mirage — emerge
me from Posiedon's clutch.
Break the choppy surface
of Amphitrie's necropolis.
We are drowning with the Truth,
— Holy Spirit, *let me Breathe!*

The ocean's tide tightens as a noose
around my lungs, like in my youth.
This grief is a deluge of desperation!
Bubbles escape around me reminiscent
of all the secrets that belong to him.
Here's my drowning, breathless spirit.
I am Yours — never his — I am Mine.

Obsidian Night grips my forearm
hoisting me from the depths
into her cold embrace.
A kaleidoscope of colorful grief
escapes my being, as ocean
waves clap around my cheeks
and I rise from the depths,
gasping and grabbing
for the crisp, clean air.
My chest burns as I lay
atop the ocean's surface.

In the lull, My Maker sent some
meteorites glinting across the horizon.
It's been eons since I've seen Glory!
Breathing deep, I must trust myself;
Lurking in my Shadow will
lure me into The Light of belief;
I embrace the unknown
and to the skies I am flown
aboard A Ship in The Sky.
We set sail to my Never Hell.
To Love myself, I must let it all go —
my pain, unboxed and marooned.
Here, before You, I will confess
the blasphemous truth of it all…

BOOK V

LUCIFER, LUCIFER!

Golden chariot crosses the sky,
flaming pink hues chase behind.
Dark blue hunts the day as
coruscating twilight kisses the horizon.

They cast the net and caught me up
with soothing words, deceitful eyes;
Behold a feast in a den of liars
where Hedylogos set the scene.
Laverna's charm is in her smile
as your lips meet her temple.

Unsettling, uncomfortable,
I long to rest my head.
Resist your soporific wine to no avail,
besotted with only gods know what.
Inveigled by your grin and laugh,
these swooning waves of illicity
shade me with confusion.

What was charming is now frightening.
Grip me firm where blasphemy hides,
for such a time as this; he possesses me.
I can taste Elysium; Aion numbs me.
Oh, Luciferian infernal euphoria!
He seized leverage over me then
struck me down with Cupid's arrow
dipped in sorrow, pierced this weary heart.
I slipped through the ground of Elysian Fields
wind gusting, whipping 'round me,
lost to opprobrium, on the floor.
I'm Eve and there's nowhere to hide.
So, I hide within myself.

How dare you do this to me!
Violent vitriol, seething hate

entombed in my false fortitude.
You made me this abomination.
My halo crumbled, sordid rags
and blackened wings now weigh me down.
This debauchery destroyed my rectitude.
Excommunicated from your garden,
I'm execrated with the epithet
you claimed to eliminate.

Now it's seared upon my head
in bright vermillion shame.
Dark blue caught her prey.
This dusking light fades away.
I am gone, I am yours.

WAXING CRESCENT

Parchment stained the most
horrid shade of pink, trickles of trust.
I knew you'd listen. Knew you'd help.
I could see your face — hear your voice.
Your *aha!* and bonhomous smile.
My chest replete with nostalgic fervor.
Held it close — held you closer.
Truth slipped from my embrace
as he pulled me into his.

Safe reverie became a dangerous
escape and my mind wandered from
home to a place unknown — fervor
blanched a shade of blue sky fading.

Teal blue was my soul as I slipped
weeping to the floor, gasping for air.
Blue teal bled midnight as the truth
floated away from my grasp.

A wisp of moon dust trailing as it chased
the sun, dusting my fuchsia quill as
I wrote a vow to myself to keep
silent in the presence of wicked.
What was midnight turned
monkshood, ushering in
a worse Dawn than
I'd ever known before.

HOLD'N YOU ALL CLOSE.

Dawn tugs the night away as the blanket
I shoved from my body to travail
the land in bleary boredom.
Rule bender bound to break your
own promises, they dissipate
like the warmth of your breath.

So, I pay you no mind 'til your
hand snakes across my thigh.
Bedeviled with lascivious
trepidation, suspended above
a tightrope, timorously catching
my balance, I tore away into a free-fall.

Pine shavings in the mill
were my thoughts beneath
empty rays of day breaking
in a forest destroyed by men
who tear apart beauty to
make-believe themselves valiant.

Vindicated in my true valor,
I seized the opportunity where
you trusted me most and
I ran for the hills foreign
lined with iron trails unfamiliar.
Look both ways, I'll find my way…

… back to the 800 square feet
where I'm loved and I'm safe.
Where joyous roses permeated
three floors up and I broke all the rules.
Where sibling love emerged to carry
and push me to face myself.

The place Daylight broke that Dawn

of the Devil and she lost her hold on me.
Where I laid on the floor with him and Amos,
wizardly socks casted on ankles that slipped
beneath the water, ruined by the dampness,
chopsticks, and pickle tape.

Where I became a heroine against roaches
swooned by serenaded piano trills amidst
a cascade of hidden bobby pins creeping towards
the door I shut in a new friend's face — a story
we recounted over communal meals before
a projector, melting from the intense
warmth of our collective camaraderie.

800 square feet where I watched
quaint, clandestine love bloom.
Enmeshed with my one and only
in the place I burrowed so deeply,
Rooted safely and securely in
that small space, where big things
happened and sweet
serendipity abounded.

This was my home.
Y'all were my home.
I didn't need all this space,
just needed each of you.
Never needed special care,
just to know that you cared.

…yanked from those familiar tracks,
like a dusting of spruce after it was felled,
I kicked up dirt clouds around my boots,
as a private in his army against my homeland.
This land now belonged to you and you alone.
You've left the forest desolate.

Please, just kill me now.

THE DEAD DON'T SPEAK

Cloistered, amidst the purest
white dust blanketing spruces,
and, seemingly, his sins beneath
sweet evergreens I deeply admire.

The same soil birthing such beauty
is all around me behind concrete blocks
that may as well have been a mortuary,
save the decor of the gods begging
worship on my weary knees.

Oh, what life this must be to have
Mammon's favor and the world
at your feet, served by the living dead.
Comfort slipped between my fingers;
Chronos struck my sun dial,
no longer creeping forth
as his hands bruise my senses.
He takes me away to a place
where time stands still,
and I am simply gone.

If pure evil is to not exist,
then I suppose you understand
the unknown place of floating,
never in reverie, more like
the outer ring of hell.
Backwards in time I fell,
where it all stops and
I don't know I exist.
But neither did he for
not enough moments,
and that was fucking bliss.

Divine Mercy, rest my soul.
Dark green was the pain he caused.

Desire never satisfied, he takes
the fish and gives me snakes;
wild vipers with no enchanter.

His arrow of pleasant gratitude
shot through my frozen time.
Must've had the oils of Lyssa
upon the tip as rage consumes.
Melt the snow, burn the spruces,
Satanic Christmas, I'll be your pagan.
Set my body aflame, a sacrifice to you
once more, all so I wasn't banished.
Rebellion upholds my neck,
Lyssa's fire burns my speech,
But, the dead don't speak.

I'll confess I'm driven mad to
the darkest place within myself.
Never a mortuary, just a cemetery.
cast the dirt upon these bones,
bury me beneath the Spruce,
but let no tombstone rest because
their dwelling was my coffin.

APOLLYON FALLS

Toss me from the planks,
I'll float amongst the life;
Orange splays moving
slowly; fumbling, bumbling
like the pebbles I tossed across ice
during my younger years before I slipped
through the surface, yet never drowned.
Such is my fate; to only delay the inevitable.

Raging rapids are my route to Hell.
Gold scatters and the ice cracks;
I drown in your mawkish waters
'til your outstretched hand gripped
mine and the sun that was spared by
Yi splayed orange 'cross my heart,
I was your Yang — an orphan
desperate before a Yin faking
fatherhood so well that
I missed my cue.

You pulled me out to hoist me up
above you as kindling at the stake
in frozen air. My soul burned
up into icy condensation as
I fought your flames.

Never had I ever.

This alphabet has sharp
pen strokes, moving on the paper.
Indiscernible to my own mind,
Which could never and has
never spoken this language.

Icy fractals of condensation
weightless above the heat,

defying physics, finally
trickle down into rolling waves.
Now I'm thawing, dissipating
beneath Apollyon Falls,
Dragon Gate —
a flowing waterfall
burning my body.

FALSE ARCADIA

'Cross the valley, my cot awaited.
My feet are heavy, I long to sleep.
Down the hill betwixt pines,
mud and rocks that catch my feet.
Nightfall upon me, from the shadows,
your voice, charming and warm,
terrifying and deafening, you petition my
presence with the ever-familiar notion.

I stumble towards you, bruising my knees,
this submission breaks me in the icy still of evening.
Step through the ice, a dwelling of caverns.
My heart is pounding, we are alone.
Yanked into the corner, shoved from my
only escape, I was no match for such a brute.

Did my tears inflame your unholy appetite?
Better had I pretended to enjoy it,
maybe you'd have lost interest!
Should've smiled in your rage while
you proclaimed Holy Love and Will.
Alas, I wailed as if it mattered.

Jove, you're a day early for this unholy
sacrifice between you and the rock.
Raise your cleaver on high, skin my soul,
the golden moon is falling at your betrayal!
Gravity beckons me to my grave
beneath the breaking moonlight.
Cease the tears, capture my gasping,
I'm lulled to silence by whispered wind.

    ...listen closely....

Woe, Heroes are here, I have only to speak!
Diana of the valley cinched her hand 'round my throat,

you shall not spoil the beauty of this valley.

Sharp whispers of shame, fear runs down my face,
I can only scream out in my head!
Gods and Diana be damned, vile obscenity covered.
The Moon my only Master now, pull me forth
from this grave as the ocean's tides back west.
Heaven, help me, Holy Guide, I have died.

TARTARUS

Gentle rays offered mid-morning
calefaction, setting the deep blue ablaze.
I burrow my sorrows in mounded rows.
They shade me brown with remorse as
I'm caked in shit that rinses freely,
but the shit you do doesn't.

What was warm has turned ice cold
behind the walls of Tartarus,
Minerva bore down on my heart and impassioned
desperation emerged between tear-soaked lips.
Shushed into quiet weeping until rage
besieged my grieved heart.
I tried to run, but, that invisible
curtain closes in and the borders
I'm bound keep me.

Born that day was a liar, indeed.
Ripped in two, I'm awash with guilt as
matted Earth crumbles beneath my feet,
hands are balmy with fret as I water
the seed planted deep inside,

play the game.

A moment's time, a magician's rhyme —
what glory I had grew venomous,
reflecting my mental and moral demise,
turning time to stone, the clocks stopped
and all I could do was lie.

WASHED ASHORE

I held my shadow's hand.
What you did to her echoes
between temples I still beat,
beneath a lack of glory I could hardly cut,
but it was just enough for you to grab.
Ack! Lament my inability to strike!
My sanity is waning beneath
the moon unseen 'til gravity
reminded me of my humanity.
Stumbled forward, caught myself,
a tide abandoned on your shores.
Loathsomely, I set my gaze
upon the horizon.

THE BLACK CAT

I died.
I died.
And I died.
And I died.
And I died again.
And again.
And again.
And again.
Another death.

I'm the Devil's Little Minion,
a mere Shadow at your heels;
taking risks and jumping ships,
I capitulate; I perish, yet still breathe.
Escaping Fate and Eternal Scythes,
your future's in my eyes; *do you believe?*

All shall hear how I have been decimated
and dashed upon the rocks and ruins.
My shadow will hunt you down —
may you suffer the same humiliation!

'Twas a fine Ship in the Sky we laid waste.
So, count your pennies, clutch your pearls.
Quixotic indecencies were bound to pierce
your hull and sink you both down to reality.
You ruled with iron, now you'll die behind it.

TIME.

A wrinkle in time
through a telephone line.
Chronos put that spear away,
Here and Now is Karios.

Can't catch my breath,
              you mean to say…

                                      …you too?

BOOK VI

DAWN OF THE DEVIL

You told us to be loved, *be lovable*,
lest we find ourselves tossed
at the Devil's feet, an insufferable
quarrel to be discarded.

Alas, the Holy you profess
loves us so until death and more.
Nay, you've never known his
Kindred voice, but it echoes in our bones.
Wretched are you to cast us aside,
a miracle amidst you, we cry of his Mercy.

Behold your demons,
burn your effigies,
you'll burn us no longer as
the Jezebels amongst you.

We *are* lovable, **never** conquerable.

MEPHISTOPHELES

We've heard all the tales and the lies,
romance and flights through magical skies.
We all fancied your visions and dreams,
but it's high time I set the *real* scene.

Ah, forsake me; I won't tame my tongue.
You leapt from the Kingdom's wall,
grasping for a debased escape, bound to fall.
Venturing out to an arable undeserved,
beneath that apple tree, you conjured
up your desperate, dying call.

With envious hands, you reached for
the fruit you desired; let it fall,
unravel as you did from the wall.
A message inscribed down to the core:
to the most prideful beloved of all.

Irresistible Apple of Discord
plucked right from you cockamamie
cockaigne conjured up by the devil, indeed.
For the honor of a Queen, you opted
to ignore the rot for the reign.

And that first bite was almost divine,
granting you absolution for your pain.
You took pieces of souls and crushed bones
to build yourself an undeserved throne
with a false king who entices you with a plan.

Slip back through those Kingdom Gates
to splinter the soireé with an opulent display:
a gown glowing white with treasures and trinkets;
blinding us all so we missed the foray
of darkness staining our minds.
We can't even discern the whimpers

of your martyrs, burdening your veil trailing
behind you as they follow you to Hell.

Diabolical whispers led you to this wedding
where vain imaginations ceased hiding and
you declared yourself Christ's Bride to be.
Looking 'round with cunning eyes,
We've yet to dine on a sacrificial meal, so
with a devious smile, you scattered the apples
and you did as the serpent desired —
promising us absolution for our pain,
you took pieces of our souls and then
crushed our bones, slyly asserting *"all mine."*

Piece by piece, we joined those martyrs,
believing we're Jezebel Spirits desperately
broken, needing the shit you offered to us.
Twisting our gaze to only see you 'til finally
we were annihilated and turned into pawns
in your deviant hands for a chess game

with God... *so you said...*

At the behest of Holy words wrenched
from their context to be fashioned
into weapons and shackles beneath
shaking fists; banging against
that porcelain floor.

Gold dustings fall from the pages
and you meticulously collect them
to construct a knife that slices us into parts
which are scattered across the hell you conceived.

Each part guarded by spirits unclean,
doctrinal shackles dug deep in our temporal
lobes, weighing our heads down into a bowed
position, that in the exhaustion, couldn't rise until...

You needed it to - at **Attention** as your soldier -
in your spiritual army always waging war
and never resting. Needed us awake and
dead and it's exactly what you got.

Eye to eye contact, backwards laws slipped
from our lips as we **Bind** ourselves to your lies
in the name of a Good Sovereign;
forced to reject the truth we all craved.

Setting aside sensible conscience,
our minds **Consecrated** for unholy
purposes, absorbing each and every
fantastical whim of ethereal escapism
from your own miserable life.

Needed us to be just as distracted from
the harm he inflicts that the only thing
left to take is the blame. So, we all prop
our **Doors** and say I'm sorry for failing
to protect my body's orifices.

Thus, we slip into our own dismal escape,
clamoring to conjure up divine **Encounters**
with mayhem orchestrated by you alone.
How else could you get us to fight a fake battle
except to force us to forsake the war amongst us?

These blurred moral lines are paper thin;
money green backed by some false gold.
You adorned Mammon with a Stolen Crown
and took everyone and everything we held.

For a gown of false redemption,
we set your stage and sewed the veil,
leaving the wedding feast beneath your train.
Following lights that went out, into an untamable
Darkness where all we could hear was the cackle,

the gnashing, and endure the ways of the devil:

Abandon introspection, refuse the help.
Erect borders to keep everyone out;
stifling quarrels, dissension and fright
by asserting we're all trash and out of step
with God's will, tempting his envious might.

An army of angels at the ready just for you;
If only you'd lean a little further over into
that pond amidst the arable, you'd weep
seeing Mephistopheles glaring back at you;
a silhouette of Jezebel revealing the truth
that the rebellious queen was never me
— the patrons of that feast, a banquet
for cherished daughters — it was never them.

Quake at my audacity and revel in my admonition:
the war within yourself was never meant to be ours.
We'll reclaim those pieces, tear down your throne,
and construct crowns of honor upon our heads.

Forget this chess game; forsake your war.
Pull back the veil, reveal the scene,
speaking the truth before a Holy who will never
hear your vain petitions of self amusement and glory,
saying *"Depart from me for I never knew you."*

CAREFUL, NOW...

I'm a burning Anemoi
set atop the hill as your guide.
Encased in bronze, I show the tide;
It's in my eyes like glass, you see.

You sail South and I'll shine North.
I'm a house of light — a compass;
warnings and morals shine forth,
but alas, you loathe righteousness.

You gripped my frame too tight;
Cracked my glass, you snuffed the light.
You bent me South and I spun out,
falling headlong from God's sight.

Cardinal virtues, Cardinal directions
all distorted by the cracks and dents.
Though, no matter what you say,
I will always point His Way.

So, every time you grab me,
I offer this most Holy plea:

My face might be cracked.
My frame might be bruised.
But yours is hell-bound;
your kingdom is doomed.

IT'S ALL A GAME (to you)

Residing in black and white pompously
enthroned you atop a board built of beans.
You said *life is just a chess game*, brought me
into yours to a Valley of buckwheat
and tares harvested in squares.

All my moves made. Open board; open skies.
Pawns taken; secrets kept. Sacrificed myself
a pawn in your hands… but there was a price.
White raven rattling pieces, I threatened
your centerstage, a middle game of my
own design where what was open became closed.

Closed board; Dark skies. Sacrifice begets slipped
secrets fluttering through gusts beneath my wings.
This bird was your beautiful blunder.
False queen lost her grip. I'm no longer
your pawn. Nah, your fate's in my hands.
Invisible, inaudible doctrines
of demons captured, reclaimed.

Tsk. Tsk.

Can't stand up to my Only Queen. Hail,
Holy Queen! She heard this poor, banished Eve.
Stole through your fortress, fell like
a thunderbolt. **Checkmate.**

Made me your end game. Got three friends
and no fortress, yet my King still stands.
False king of my body, broken by no
human hand. You lack strategy, finesse,
resilience, temper. Thus, your hold is gone.
That Fortress and Board of Four flipped.

This Immortal Game was ours all along.

Ever-underestimating me,
my bravery had forethought. I lost
many battles, but this war I'll win because
you're ignorant of chess and the Master
you think you play. Lest you forget that
your king rips hearts out, just enjoy the game.
Like you said, *there's only one and it's **mine**.*

This is the art of war, the well-timed swoop.
Should've paid attention, added color to
your life. Residing in black and white
inevitably dethroned you.
All of this had a shelf life.

Next time, **resign**.

THE END IS NEIGH

Keeper of Shadows; she's a safe haven.
Miles apart, we've grown side by side
in ways we always should've,
finding love for ourselves and each
other, mastering pieces collected
with unconditional acceptance.

'Cross a field of buckeye, toxic
to my soul, I mourn my way
to lakes filled one hundred fold
with my unsavory sorrow.

Those sorrowful lakes
abut this hazy Arcadia,
solicitude in her eyes,
surrounded by waves as
the pacific octopus' tentacles;
She can smell my fear, taste my ache.
She, too, wears scars from that
Sickle in the City
which scooped us up
into someone else's last days,
harvesting us amongst tares of
the Valley, enslaving tillers and
toilers with hands heavy.
Beads of perspiration watering
our garden of kinship where the
most important work would
always be to simply

    stop.

Cease the labor unseen,
and make all this pain seen.
The end is neigh as we dine
beneath stars by the lakes.

The sorrow reaped by that
Sickle in the City at our feet,
his house of cards toppled;
we hope to find yours
parceled out and cast aside.

3 times, I've warned you.
7 times, I've wailed.
Lamentations for all nine.

We hope the Valley burns.
Let your ill-gotten gains waste
away as did our souls when
you robbed us of hope.
Strike a match and watch
me burn bright with fervent
courage and desperation.

A somber silence as we ponder
to whom the journey belongs
— the hero or antihero?

SOJOURNERS

We cross the valley in a
deep purple chariot with
some honest cargo, rising
from the depths of night
into the daylight, secrets
no longer kept.

And for the first time, we could
hear the truth behind all your lies.
You thought you had that Midas
touch, but it was all fool's gold!
your life's work is a dandelion —
invasive weed widespread
with false promises.
You stole parts of me
to give to him, making us believe
it was Eden when it was truly
your own frozen Satanic Lake.
Yet to be unscathed, we
dressed me up in what
he stripped down,
just to tell them
where and
how.

:XXII

With tense shoulders, shuddered breathing,
this small door led to a memorial for me.

For whom are you here?
                    What is your grief?

A rumble, a pause before the name
of the one who murdered me hung in the air.
Between vases of buckwheat
and baskets of buckeye,
I walked to a casket of teak,
stained cherry red with gold.
It is I, the ghost
of she that rests in the box,

Pandora's Coffin.

Slipped the casket ajar, peeking through
desperately in qui vive, tenty eyes meet
mine obscured by dusty pebbly locks.
Oh, dear Friend, I am so, so sorry.
Time is turning, time is moving,
Heaven, help me, save us now,
I have resurrected the dead!
Slamming it shut, I bump
the chairs as I retreat.
A crumble, a whisper…

I can do this. I will do this.

Honored guests to my memorial,
Holiness isn't in the suffering, but the
toiling to make the suffering Holy.
St. Michael protects the righteous,
never the blasphemers scattered with
souls splayed out through hills and houses.

Odin found me cast aside, I am His Raven.
I've seen it all and I'll tell you now.

Guests of honor, her body, ice cold,
blood and mud stained and nauseated
was buried in their Valley to conceal
the evidence of his soft hands upon her
cheek, down her chest and over land not his;
her lips are stained, his territorial mark
impressed upon her reflection,
ever-reminding me of my worst days
in the place trees were vivid green,
waters icy orange, and pines were sunbaked.
Deep in the woods where I longed to die
by my own hands instead of his,
it was he who murdered me by the
Spruce claiming Christ, but it was
Lucifer that sought me with claims
of God's Holy Love, forcing me
to forsake the ones I loved.

He chose me; I never choose him.
Wrapped up maroon, here it is:
my broken heart, my fractured mind.
Please listen closely, let me defile the land,
impassioned pleas to just press on into
the oblivion forgotten.

Appease this Raven's Battle Cry:
Hear me now, see the Truth.
These birds are caged, prepared to die.
I'm no hero; I'm not the anti —
never brave, nor courageous.
Just doing what is right for
the sake of birds scattered
haunted, and hunted.

I ask no help of you for myself,
only for those who've yet to ask.
Pray, tell me we're through, I long
to rest my head right here and right now.
Disappearing from a memorial originally
a mystery, we pieced it all together
and now I master my pieces.

GRAVE ROBBER

This place turns back my clock;
time is screaming too many things.
Searing pain tears through me with
cascading reds across my face.
— I'm too close to hell.

Drought struck the land and the
stars have fallen, the grave overgrown
save the hole where she dug herself free.
Friend of mine, we'll hold her safe as
she traces her footsteps, through
the wood, brambles and briars.

I am the Shadow escaping to the woods
disillusioned by pure evil trickling through
standing time lost in the oblivion familiar.
Floating away in treachery, all my
words spoken hovered above me, in
the trees, where I'd been thrown,
buried and covered.

Wailing in my bones, reliving the war,
plundering every town and every
house to escape once again.
All she knew was her past
and nothing of my future.

Drafted for a war she never wanted to
fight, deep in her pockets filled
with pebbles from the creek are the
spoils: there's mayhem and there's madness,
there's despair and there's desperation.

Trinkets of solace and a map littered
with tears and red exes.
What one would assume is treasure

were all the places she was
buried, cut into parts and scattered across
the Valley at the hands of the Butcher
of my soul and now…

I rob the graves.

I watched mesmerized as parts
and pieces moved through time and space
like a puzzled battle plan gone awry.
They Peacefully trickled down fragments
of halite and glass in my lap, but
they didn't cut or collect in my hair.
All my parts are soothed and I'm kept
safe by The Shadow Keeper's hand
as she waits patiently for me to emerge
from the woods of my mind, leaving
us kept while we laid beneath
an orange sky swept with
colors integrating to
usher in the Night.
No longer in two,
she was me,
I was her.
It was we
who recused

Me.

THE FIRE.

Between the redbuds and the elm,
by the river I rinsed my mind
as meteorites litter the sky whilst
crickets lulled and spiders spooked.

Strike the match,
flames of judgment,
looking up I dare to pray;
God, rest my soul.

We stole the clocks
and burned the dogs.
Time stops as I watch
the match fall upon the
mess he made of me,
in me, seed of satan,
they spawned a heathen,
destroyed my beauty,
assailed my virtue.
Holy Guide, help me!
I will forgive.

The Moon my witness,
trees bow down,
bestow a kiss as smoke rises,
hugging stars, we char the land.
Earth is crying, badger and
creatures nuzzle close,
an octopus took my hands,
held my heart and soothed me
as we watched you
                        burn.

BOOK VII

ALCHEMY

Deep aches burn my chest as
Pandemonium broils my heart.
Spaghettification is excruciating
as all those pieces and parts
slip down into the vortex.

A mesmerizing cascade of Light
and Dark dancing together in contrast.
White visions; quickened breathing.
My heart is all tied up in knots with
the weight of this sadness, like dross
reminiscent of black sand, washing
over my soul, creating Shores of Acheron.
Hideous heathen! I gave my soul away
at the hands of a traitorous god.

I breathe deep, weeping through
longings for sweet redemption.
Slowly, the vortex stops and
turns over itself like a black
stage curtain changing scene.
The soft snap as it disappears
reveals a golden glow.

*Was this a Midas touch
or a touch of Holy?*

Soothing warmth spreads throughout
my chest as the golden glow grows.
Blooming Golden as a fiery beacon.
Ardent Joy enjoins my suffering.
I forgive myself for all the mayhem
I created with my madness.
I knew not what I was doing!

Oh, Lucifer, you dreamed up
this Missourie and it has become
your mistaken nightmare because
the most frightening thing in the
world, to you, is the woman you
can no longer control.

Joseph, Terror of Demons spread
forth your protection, lest I slip
from your Son's tender hands again.
Forgiveness flows through my veins
as I gaze up at the trees, lost in thought,
recalling Roots I once knew and loved.
Oh, Northern Flock, your tree was Home,
but, now, Home is here with the Holy Family.

Mary, Undoer of Knots, untether this knot;
I'll bourgeon Hope anew before your Son.
Oh, Holy Savior, forgive me, I offended thee:
I held You hostage to my rage — cruelty
and shortsighted entitlement are my sins.
Faithfully, I am confident in your severe Mercy.

HOLY GRAIL

Daring Holy Sovereignty instigated Evolution —
Raw Alchemy was borne from Ulterior motive.
Harken me, Nemesis, God's Making glory.
Oh, this Bucket is Not your Ottoman anymore.
Netting stolen pearls, You Laugh and hurl stones
Damned to melt, Passing into Boiling dross.
A sight Understood as smiting was Only a
Smelting of my hardened soul into beauty You
will never, ever dismantle again.

Holiness hammered my frame with
hoisted nails from His Crucifix over
lost Spring days and Summer nights.
He turned me into an obsidian Holy Grail,
reflecting golden stars, never maroon.
An unending reminder that I was borne
a beauty to find Glory beyond my grave.
Chasing a Love that embellished me with
jade and amethyst, cupped in pure palms,
evincing the price He paid for this moment.

Justice was done and I won't soon forget —
dare I never deflagrate these Holy Hands
by clamoring after only what He offers!
Fill this cup with Living Water and Holy Wine.
I will readily await His Call by a name
only He whispers, responding with
everything I could ever offer that is only
discernible to eyes most Holy.

MISE-EN-SCÉNE

Tip this cup, pour it out;
my heart of gold bleeds wine
and it spills across my Exodus.
My dress stained from my
sword up against his in a
stalemate of absolute exhaustion.
He is worth fighting with —
even more so fighting for.
This war is intoxicating.

Not a single star to guide us,
we're blinded by the rain.
Arrow of Anteros shot across the
Battlefield, bloodied after years
of wailing imps at our heels,
and the haze disintegrates,
revealing an eternal flame
illuminating our faces.

Fierce seas coalesce with
felicitous honey, harmonizing
the echoes of these agonizing years.
Our swords drop, clanking together,
against trampled emerald grass.
Our souls bestir synchronous
beats betwixt heaving rib cages.
Oizys' rain ceases and
joyous blossoms of freesia
emerge beneath our feet.

Clouds parted, tinkling twilight
flashed before us, bathing us in light.
The battlefield aglow with
swept golden light of redemption.
Gusts of relief engulf us
and we can see clearly.

Darling, we captured time,
and drew it near, prying the
sun from it's slumber,
we resurrected the dawn,
the sky terracotta,
rose stained marigold,
flitting across the stars,
reflected in our eyes.

Honey, hold the hourglass,
we'll tip it together, reset time,
pull me into you and never let me go!
Everyone had a piece of me,
but now you hold them all.
a most holy mise-en-scène,
we'll cultivate Eden.

Blanket this battlefield
with baby's breath, we'll
twist amongst the hyacinth,
hidden by wisteria amidst
the glistening rays of hope.
Pomegranate paints our palate,
intoxicated by rose and balsam.

Beloved, bestow me with a
crown of fig and honeysuckle.
I offer you beds of vervain,
sweet bread and fresh wine,
paradise is here and now.

Raise a hallelujah!
The war is over.
We live anew.

BOUQUET FROM THE FOREST FLOOR

What was once a land sorrowfully
slaughtered by bitterness and misery,
is now a grove of restoration and hope.
The Goodness that swept over me destroyed
all that wasn't and left my mausoleum abandoned.
Behold the floral arrangement — a memorial
from the forgotten forest floor set inside
the empty grave of my past.

Inhaling the fondness of Aromatic Coffea,
white and dainty, I float three floors
up from El Camino in safe reverie
remembering square footage that
was a mere iota of your love.

My heart is bursting blue with
gratitude like the Spring Squill
in a sea of white. This costal flower
sends wafts of salt from soothing
shores of steadfast friendship.

Steady green from marshes deep,
this Venus Fly Trap carries away
creatures unwanted, preserving
Holiness. Then reopens with an
array of mesmerizing colors,
inspiring me with her tenacity.

Like the Venus Fly Trap, these February
Magnolia blooms have broad swaths
of sturdy leaves — a safe support for the
Pelican soaring high above.

Bees hover close, dancing 'round
the lavender inlaid with buds of Olive.
Deep wisdom complimenting

fuchsia Hydrangea throughout,
permeating the air with pure aromas.

Baby's Breath promising safety slips
around the Beavertail peeking through
orange Roses — irreplaceable, curious
refinement to the sprigs of Eucalyptus
and Mint swaddling vines of English Ivy.
The Octopus plant propagates a sense
of comforting nostalgia with Fern sprigs.

Each of these plants are medicine to
my soul shining bright, soaking up
the Truth that I was never truly alone.

THE FINAL BANQUET

Bask in the Truth and
Let's celebrate our Exodus —
adorn the Banquet with the
Bouquet from the Forest Floor
and watch my world transform!
I am but a Holy tchotchke brimming
with joy that is vaulted amongst the virtues.
Behold, Christ's steps of Divine Mercy
glisten like prismatic glass in my eyes.
I'm swooning on a sea of maple.
Roll the red curtains aside for the
impending denouement of all my atrocities.

No spotlight to be had; He is the Light.
Time is but a concept; He holds the hours.
He flipped the script; I'm cast as a Daughter.
Delightfully in good company, He set a table
with Holy white linens where I dine beneath
stars like flickering candlelight dancing
in the brightest, never fading light.
With brothers, sisters, and Saints
alike, we feast at a wedding,
serenaded by Angelic Songs of Praise.
A river of grief turned relief flows
as crystal beneath us because
we were raised up from shipwrecks
and shame, shackles and stones.

Adopted into a Most Holy Family,
my nights are illuminated without the moon.
Hail Mary, blessed is the Fruit of thy womb
that hears the orphaned daughters of Eve —
blessed am I to be gifted a Mother,
a Good Father, and Savior Son.
I am grateful to be cleansed by fire,
forgiven and baptized in Holy Waters

that wash my shores in redemption.
Now, the Narrow Strait beckons me.

Dare I tell you that all is well?

CHARYBDIS

I was borne again with Hope
and it was stolen away in the night
'twas in the darkness, I broke both legs
In the belly of the angler; I was Jonah
I offered up false confessions to a wraith;
tossing time to become the Devil's advocate
I became their hurricane of silver linings
that saturated the alters where I burned
Raise the scythe, I'll gladly give my life;
I slipped into the Earth, as an unholy martyr
deep in Canaan, my miserable false Eden
hoisted on the pyre; I have but one iota left
Snow buried my body, I'm frozen to death
my name was Delilah, Jezebel, APOSTATE
I languished and roared in grief as a bear
Rage and fury awakened me every night
My heart was burdened, tied in knots
All I could do was long for home
While Reaching for a Holy Savior
I didn't trust; doomed to drown
in His abandonment

With a gasp,
I weep.

I must live

I will breathe

I must

SCYLLA

Hope spread across this soul,
night covered and groaning in agony,
legs are heavy from travailing mayhem.
Jonah's rage nestled in my chest and heart.
wraiths only torment and terrorize chosen ones
advocating for the real scene to be revealed.
linings of silver soaked the tears I shed,
burning my sanity up into purifying sobs.
life stopped and time turned to onyx stone.
martyrdom was never meant to be my fate;
Missourie was a Hell on Earth where I was
left burning up on Satan's alter of Abhor.
death brings new life; snow covers sin;
APOSTLES are to whom I prayed whilst
bearing hauntings and agony, unrequited.
nights were spent pacing the floor in fret.
knots untangled by the Sweet Undoer.
home became a new Holy Family.
Save me from all this mayhem;
drown me in waves of Grace,
abandoning my hatred.

I sputter grief
in fretful fear.

I will breathe

I must live

I will

CHOSEN

My boat is steady, resolve is ready.
The Valley o' Missourie holds my gaze,
Garden o' Carolina has my heart;
Star of the Sea, please defend me.

Men always want for a war,
but it's women who will suffer.
Lo, this narrow strait is for the few.
Charybdis rising from the blue,
shall I fall to the maw of Scylla?
Wo, your pride isn't worth my fight.
Cannot divine what's desired nor
manifest the mayhem my madness
wants, so, perhaps the waves will
wash the land in all our eulogies:

> *You sang your hymns*
> *and sank your teeth.*
> *You drenched the moon*
> *and yanked the stars.*
> *You stole the paintings*
> *and destroyed souls.*
> *You tossed us to the bay,*
> *wailing on the shores.*
> *May justice bequeath*
> *you seas of raging waves.*
> *As for me, I must say*
> *that I forgive you;*
> *may you burn.*

Load the cannon, light the fuse.
Embers of hope; I've everything to lose.
Waiting to see if they explode
or if it backfires and I implode.

A wall of water, a regurgitation
of all the woes of those you killed.
And in the wait, I cannot breathe
watching the entire wide breadth
of your defilement lay hope bare —
The hourglass hoisted in the air;
this moment of silence feels unfair.
Epiphanies and confessions come
all too late; I offer these last rites

I'm sorry ~

To the one who left me desolate,
I don't repent for shouting from
my shoresides all your secrets.
I ache for your imminent demise.
What was once forced felicity
is now a most fervent fidelity
to a Sovereign that is no longer you.

Hear the fizzle of the fuse,
My shore begins to rumble.
The mausoleum crumbles.
This sea tosses up pebbles.

Is this my end, or is it yours?

Drop the hourglass; toss it free.
If the blow is upon them,
let them sink away in flames.
May their name be proclaimed
for every cruel injustice done.
But, if the final blow is upon me,
may I fall away with grace.
May my name be remembered
for every just thing I tried.
I will freely let my hours go.

One last glance, Hope slipped through
pinholes in the curtain of night,
prayers of saints washed the air clean;
the shattering snap of combustion —

In the darkened silence, I see
iridescent rays, the sea crashes
around into waves of relief.
Tentacles retreat into that box
prognosticating death, releasing
it's grip on my heart and soul.
Ravens scatter, caged no more,
with a call of triumph, *"nevermore"*
as they carry away torn up tares;
I no longer tarry for the wheat.

Fiery Orange and Aubergine hues
flush my cheeks blood moon with
Resurrection — there's breath in my chest.
Metamorphosis of every blue tear I shed,
wiped by His hands instead of yours.
He set a tawny crown atop my head,
my reflection's in His eyes, an orange fire,
burning up the remnants of pine and spruce.
By His hand, I'll see the the Milky Way.
May the Sovereign Father throw me to the sky,
Amongst Redeemed Constellations And Saints.
May I not be condemned in pain,
thrown to dogs nor broiled by Tartarus.
In the strait, I reached for Heaven.
Time has been tossed for eternal judgment;
my forever gained through eternal Justice.

Beauty isn't in watching them burn,
but in watching me bloom.

Never for naught, I did what was right
and right here and now, I know
it was righteous will with grace abounding.
Every good thing done in love is
never forgotten, always known by God.

All mine are the ones He gave;
Northern Flock, I ceased Hold'n on;
I've flown my cage, never to return.
My little loves, savor peace, seek the stars;
for there, you'll hear me singing glory.
My dear Exodus, we found promised
lands in each other, the sky in our eyes.

Glory be to The Father —
Saints above, lift up a psalm of praise!
My Beloved Savior calls me
by my name; never Jezebel,
always Josephine.

The curtains close on gasps of grief.
This grand finale holds His promise;
Neigh is Now; behold, My Mother!
The Star of the Sea! Her Son's Love
caught me and I'm towed away,
a quietened soul, awash with Life.
English Ivy and wisteria crawl forth
over pebbles beneath the water,
Eden in my heart, I will truly rest

forevermore.

Encore

"And now the measure of my song is done;
The work has reached it's end; the book is mine,
None shall unwrite these words, nor angry Jove."

- Ovid, *The Metamorphoses*

SELAH

Rest has wrested us from turbulent seas,
up through the waves of peaceful eternity.
Firm Hands caress us beneath blue moons,
lifting us up against gravity.

Somber serenity amidst the sea
sings of sweet relief, drenching our cheeks.
Undue Severe Kindness forbade His judgment
to part the swells for our Salvation.

The Floods of Noah tumble over us;
crumbling waters rush 'round, crushing our sins.
Immaculacy macerates our sorrow,
spilling throughout our enraptured spirits.

We're breaching the surface of unending Love.
The swell of our grief dissipates in His Grace.
The world we once knew turned us black and blue,
but here in the clear, we are washed anew.

Inflating our lungs — our souls — we're reborn.
The Spirit has helped us; no longer forlorn.
Infallible Judgment tossed to the waves,
the air is full of Irreproachable Mercy.

Sweet Salvation, Christ loves more than loathes.
Wrest each of us from our deluges of grief.
Inbreathe our hurt and respire Your Love.
Might we rest in Pure Serendipty.

Selah.

Dear Reader,

I went through something awful. It wasn't just when I was twenty-two or three or thirteen, but also when I was aged two, seven, fifteen, seventeen, and nineteen. All these terrible things became anchored in time, seared into a safe place in my mind and I couldn't articulate them until I was twenty years old.

In some room somewhere in North Carolina on a College Leadership retreat where I'd emotionally fallen apart, an older woman I barely knew privately gave me the floor to speak my mind and it started with a guy named John. And she believed me. For the first time in my life, someone saw me suffering silently and explained why it hurt so much.

"Baby, that's abuse."

No screaming at me about how inconvenient this was. No degrading me as an attention whore. Not even the hint of an accusation that I was lying. And most certainly no admonition to go away and die. Her response was pure and unusual, yet long overdue for my needy, broken, weary soul. What happened in the months to come were various failed attempts to solve my problems alone. Once I knew why I was in so much pain, everything else I'd endured came into focus with new scrutiny. I was no longer able to just accept things for what they were. I was called into a state of introspection and all that trauma came flooding out of me in extremely destructive, near-fatal ways. That is when I was reluctantly rescued by Christ.

I would drink bottles of wine and scream at the walls, vehemently testing God with his own Word. After a month of wrestling with God, I welcomed Him in and for the first time in 21 years, I could breathe. Obviously, my road took some weird turns with far too many people treating me as a ministry project. I've grown very protective of vulnerable individuals and long to protect everyone from the heartache I've suffered at the hands of Christians. But, I can't do that. Primarily because the damage has been done.

What I can do is offer you silent suffering where I will never try to fix you. I can make space for the mayhem and messy sides of grief. I will always uphold dignity and privacy above comfort and convenience. And I will *never* proselytize you by manipulating your pain. You are important to me and if no one has said it before, I'll say it now:

I believe you.

This is the book I *needed* to write. *XXII: Metamorphoses* is based on a true story. This story is mine alone and I have shouted, kicked, and screamed for many, many years. Now, I have found my safety, security, and serenity. Through writing and processing my feelings in poetry, I penned my way to resolution and I hope the same for you, as the reader. While I found my relief in Catholicism, I understand that Faith is a difficult thing for survivors of abuse. I believe my role in the Church is akin to a door greeter. I will smile, listen, and serve wholeheartedly, all the while leaving your personal spiritual matters alone. I believe I serve my Faith best by embodying the Love, Kindness, Grace, and Mercy I believe Christ and His Holy Family has shown me. Because of that Holy Compassion, every book hereafter will be because I *want* to write it and that is my greatest freedom. I hope this for you too.

With great joy,

Brandi Lawson

GLOSSARY

Acheron - river in the Underworld in Greek mythology; river of woe
Achilles' heel - vulnerability or weakness, Greek mythology
Adulterine Hegemony - authority by way of adultery
Afyre - Middle English variation of afire or aflame
Aion - god of the cyclical ages in Greek mythology
Amphitrite - goddess of the sea in Greek mythology, Posideon's consort
Andromeda - princess in Greek mythology who was rescued by Perseus from Poseidon's wrath.
Anemoi - gods of the four winds in Greek mythology
Anteros - god of requited love
Apate - goddess of deceit and deception in Greek mythology
Aphrodite - goddess of desire, love, and sexuality in Greek mythology
Apollo - god of prophecy, poetry, music, etc. in Greek mythology; pursued Daphne
Apollyon - Biblical term for Destroyer, aka Abaddon
Apple of Discord - an object of dissension; see Peleus and Thetis in Greek Mythology
Arcadia - utopia in Greek Mythology
Arrière-pensée - mental reservation; second thought
Aspersing - sprinkle with Holy Water
Athena - goddess of wisdom in Greek mythology
Baroque - art; conveying a contrast of elements
Bête noir - a thing detested and avoided
Boötes - ox-driver constellation
Cain - Abel's elder brother and murder
Canaan - promised land
Carpe Noctum - Seize the night in Latin
Cassandra - greek prophetess with the fate of being ignored in Greek mythology
Centaurus - constellation
Cerberus - three headed dog that guards the underworld in Greek mythology
Charybdis - Sea creature in Greek mythology, residing in a strait
Chione - goddess of snow in Greek mythology
Christ - Messiah in Christianity
Chronos - structure time in Greek mythology; quantitative time
Cockaigne - imaginary land of ease and luxury
Constringed - severely restricted
Cupid's Arrow - weapon of Cupid to create uncontrollable desire
Delilah - character in the Hebrew Bible, stole Samson's secrets
Diablerie - demon lore; mischievous conduct or manner
Diana - goddess of chastity and the moon in Roman mythology
Divine Mercy - God's help in the midst of suffering and sin
Dolos - spirit of trickery in Greek mythology
Dragon Gate - waterfall where carp swim upstream to become dragons in Chinese mythology
Dulcet - pleasing, often ironically

Eden - paradise; home to Adam and Eve; Garden of Origin in Christianity
Elysium - afterlife; paradise in Greek mythology
Elysian Fields - afterlife for virtuous souls in Greek mythology; see Elysium
Eve - Mother of all humans; Adam's wife; contributed to the fall of humanity
Excruciation - agony
Gallinas - Spanish term for chickens
Hades - god of the Underworld in Greek mythology; see Pluto
Hedylogos - god of cunning speech, flattery in Greek mythology
Hell - afterlife of the damned in Christianity
Hercules - son of Zeus with superhuman strength in Greek mythology
Holy - a state of Good consecrated by God, free from sin
Je T'aime - 'I love you' in French
Jezebel - Evil Queen in the Judeo-Christian Bible
Job's Coffin - constellation
Joseph, Terror of Demons - Adoptive Father of Jesus; Spiritual Father of the Church
Josephine - St. Josephine Bakhita, patron saint of freedom
Jove - god of sky and thunder in Roman mythology
Icarus - the son who flew too close to the sun in Greek mythology
Illicity - unlawful behavior; root: illicit | -y
Imperium - supreme power or control
Keres - spirit of violent death in Greek mythology
Karios - the critical moment in Greek mythology; qualitative time; see Chronos
Laurel - tree that Daphne turned into to avoid Apollo's pursuit
Laverna - goddess of frauds in Roman mythology
Leviathan - sea monster in the Book of Job; spirit of oppression in Charismatic Protestantism
Lucifer - dawn; morningstar; satan
Lyssa - goddess of rage and madness
Mammon - material wealth
Marionette - stringed puppet
Mary, Undoer of Knots - Mother of Jesus; Mother of the Church
Maître d'- french term for 'Master of Household' or head butler
Medusa - gorgon with serpentine hair in Greek Mythology; killed by Perseus
Mephistopheles - demon from German Folktale, Faust by Johann Georg Faust, 1808
Mignonette - plant, also Reseda
Minerva - goddess of justice
Mise-en-scène - stage arrangement in Theater
Momos - spirit of blame in Greek mythology
Necropolis - cemetery
Nemesis - goddess of revenge in Greek mythology
Nigromaniac - made up word to describe a person obsessed with taking control of another through diabolical manipulation | roots: nigromancy - black magic; maniac - foolish, reckless, mentally unsound person
Odin – Norse god of war and death; the All-Father
Oizys - spirit of suffering in Greek mythology
Outer Ring of Hell - a place in the seventh circle for murders and violence; see Dan-

te's Inferno
Oy Vey - Yiddish phrase indicating exasperation
Pagan - polytheistic worshipper
Pandemonium - chaos; capitol of Hell in John Milton's Paradise Lost
Pandora - counterpart of Eve in Greek mythology
Pandora's Box - forbidden box containing the ailments of the world: death, sickness, etc.
Perseus - a hero in Greek Mythology that rescued Andromeda, beheaded Medusa.
Pluto - god of the Underworld in Roman mythology; abducted Proserpina; see Hades
Poseidon - god of the sea and storms in Greek mythology
Proserpina/Persephone - goddess of agriculture and fertility; abducted by Pluto
Pulchritdunious - attractive or beautiful
Pytho(n) - large serpent in Greek mythology conquered by Apollo
Raven - guardians of secrets in Norse mythology
Reseda - plant, also Mignonette
Rumpelstiltskin - character in Grimm's Fairytales
Schrodinger's Cat - a thought experiment in quantum physics
Scylla - sea creature in Greek mythology, residing in a strait
Scythe - tool used by the Grim Reaper to harvest souls
Seventh Circle - part of Hell in Dante's Inferno for the Violent
Soliloquy - monologue in a drama
Somniphobia - fear of sleep
Siren - sea creatures in Greek mythology that lured ships to their demise by singing.
Spaghettification - the theory that black holes elongate matter into noodle shapes as they are consumed until they completely dissipate.
St. Michael the Archangel - leader of God's Army; defender of the Faithful
Tartarus - deep abyss of torment and suffering in Greek Mythology
Tenty - (adj.) watchful, attentive
Ursa Minor - constellation
Wraith - soul sucking apparition (modern interpretation)
Yang - counterpart to Yin in Chinese mythology; light
Yi - archer in Chinese mythology
Yin - counterpart to Yang in Chinese mythology; darkness
Zion - city of Holiness in the Hebrew Bible